～ Absence ～

PJ Bayliss

First published 2014

1 2 3 4 5 6 7 8 9

Cover photograph provided under copywriter license from
www.shutterstock.com

ISBN: 978-0-9941090-1-9

www.pjbayliss.com

PJ BAYLISS

To all of the romantics that walk this earth and
those who dream without losing any sleep.

∿ ACKNOWLEDGMENTS ∿

I owe my debt of gratitude to a couple of dear friends who are completely responsible for igniting my passion for writing. They met me a couple of years ago and practically insisted I write poetry and short stories. With their background in the Literature industry and prior writing experience, I couldn't ignore their words of encouragement.

Throughout the past couple of years many more writers and readers have inspired me to write, but I hold these two fantastic ladies responsible for the first sparks of my imagination firing up as a writer.

B.L. Ronan

"B" is a prolifically passionate poet who has shared some soulful landscapes with her readers. Her background in the literature industry is quite impressive and when we first met she practically insisted that I write a blog to share my words.

Having that kind of encouragement from a true professional in the field became the trigger I needed to commence with my own writing. Please check her page out on Amazon.com for her book updates.

http://www.amazon.com/b.l.-ronan/e/B00CQYPVIE

Penelope Jones

Penelope is one of the most determined writers I know of. She once explained her hectic work schedule to me and I was awe inspired with her efforts. That perspective drove me to work harder on my own works.

P.S. I wrote "Precious P's Parcel" as a birthday gift for her a couple of years ago.

http://www.amazon.com/Penelope-Jones/e/B00B9MVJJO

CONTENTS

∽ FOREWORD ∽

The world changes before your eyes and behind your back. My childhood experiences were so different from my parents and from my own children. Most of which, I believe to be better in my day, because there was less drama, and more love when I grew up.

I grew up in a world that practically magnetized attitudes and behavior towards traditional conventions. Family values were a stronghold in my upbringing and there seemed to be more respect for others and their values. In a sense, my only exposure to anything outside of the norm came through music videos, late night radio stations, and my studies of artists such as Andy Warhol.

It's not as if my life was prudish neither, nor extravagant. It was just "normal" for as much as I knew what normal was all about. Nowadays though, the boundaries of normality have certainly shifted outward.

Granted, there have always been significant cultural changes between generations. Perhaps the most significant era being during the 40's and 50's with the rise of Rock 'n' Roll music, which imposed a profound impact on American culture. Music lyrics evolved to include sex, drugs, and other experiences that listeners could relate to personally. It broke through boundaries by practically celebrating issues and topics that few people were even comfortable to discuss.

Very little seems to have changed today when it comes to music and explicit lyrics. In shopping malls, we hear lyrics like this broadcasted over the radio speakers: "...*your sex takes me to paradise...*" from a song that is about a crush with celebrity Halle Berry. Here is another song lyric that became popular with tweens through the sharing of songs over social media: *"I don't mean to be pushy pushy, I'm just in it for the p**sy p**sy"*

Nothing has really changed over the years when it comes to passion and sexuality. The only thing that has changed is visibility of these sex acts was the world has become increasingly open & exposed through social media.

Consider Dominance & Submission, which has existed since the dawn of mankind with sex slaves employed by Kings and Queens throughout the world to gain control of land and exercise their authority. Roman orgies were popular 2,000 years ago. It's just that none of the action was uploaded to You Tube, Vine, or Twitter & shared with the common population.

PJ BAYLISS

So you see, human passion has existed from the dawn of time and it has been the fuel for memorable conflicts over the same period. Wars have been spawned through arguments over lovers and communities separated by the beliefs of a few. I am left with little doubt: without Passion, conflict would not exist.

In recent months, my life has been infiltrated with stories of conflict and horror through newspapers and television. I have witnessed the personal tragedies of people around the world, who are caught in the midst of a deadly battle for their basic human rights. I perceive this conflict as being fuelled by passion, despite being driven by mourning.

My previous book titled *Burnt* helped me to vent some of my frustrations and sadness of such conflict. It focused on a passion that very few people could warm up to; so now, I present the alternative passions' of **"Love and Lust"** within this piece of work titled **Absence**.

Absence is an Erotic Poetry book that reflects various perspectives of Romance, Lust, Love, and Endearment within today's ever-changing society. Given the broad spectrum of eroticism throughout the world today, I hope its content can adequately capture the diverse spirit and nature of sensuality so common throughout the world today.

"You are, and always have been, my dream."

Nicholas Sparks
The Notebook

∽ DECEMBER 2012 ∾

Dear Diary,

I have taken early leave for my seasonal holidays. Summer is here early by the look of it, and although everyone fears another drought, I am desperate to take a break. I don't mind the burnt ground crumbling underneath my feet.

The world remains in turmoil with unrest in Egypt, protests in Syria, and now satellites are being launched in North Korea prompting speculation over ICB missiles.

ICB's?
I thought those things were supposed to be extinct?

All of this anguish, violence and hatred throughout the world must surely exist through the absence of love? It is as old as human life itself, yet we still haven't learnt how to embrace it and let it flow between each other. It just seems so senseless, and I feel all so very helpless.

Helpless?…Maybe, but never useless. The least I can do is offer my own words to this equation and my perspectives on love, romance, sensuality, and lust…

∿ SONO DIPENDENTE DEI TUOI BACI ∿

With every fleeting breath,
For the rest of my life,
I simply will not forget,
Your toxin,
My strife.

With a single drop you infect,
Flowing through my veins,
A sin that I can't repent,
Your touch,
My pain.

Without mercy you intrude,
Writhing under my skin,
A sensual interlude,
Your lyric,
My sin.

With shame I may repel,
Yet I return for more,
Instinctively compelled,
Your well,
My draw.

With patience I shall wait,
Spinning wheel of destiny,
Accepting my own fate,
Your prayer,
My plea.

With cold tears flowing my cheek,
Convicted soul within my midst,
Sono dipendente dei tuoi baci,
I'm addicted to your kisses.

∾ YOU AND ME ∿

You say that you love me,
All that you can,
That I am your savior,
One and only man.

You smile when you see me,
Any time of any day,
Even though our tears,
May fall with dismay.

You tell me you need me,
Whenever we are apart,
Or when you're surrounding,
My swelling love shaft.

You reach out and grab me,
Even though I'm inside,
Deep within your loins,
With nothing to hide.

You gently caress me,
Till I sleep each night,
Before rolling over,
To cuddle me tight.

You fret when you leave me,
Shedding warm tears,
That I never look back,
Among your worse fears.

You shelter next to me,
Despite being in the dark,
Sheltered from the world,
Comforted by my heart.

∾ BATED BREATH ∾

I long to whisper your name,
Under bated breath,
In the heat of the moment,
Under sensual duress.

To scream in silence,
As you enter within,
My mound of fire,
Cavern of sin.

To holler out loud,
With my beating heart,
While our bodies collide,
Before pulling apart.

To scream in the pitch,
Of the darkest night,
As you enter my void,
Delivering my plight.

To cry out in pain,
As my tears flow free,
Mingling with my juices,
While you penetrate me.

I long to lose my innocence,
Along with my voice,
For you are my lover,
My one and only choice.

ᕫ RAPTURE ᕬ

Don't you dare deny,
My true fate or destiny,
Promise you will corrupt,
Every part of me.

Pledge your soul,
To accept me as one,
Vow not to spill,
Any portion as I come.

Unleash your passion,
With your full force,
Never let anger,
Determine our course.

Ensure I'm your one,
Your only decadent sin,
Ensure I penetrate,
Whole distance within.

Never hold back
Any portion of trust,
Consume and devour,
Every sensual thrust.

Tremble with delight,
As I implode,
Pouring deep within,
Until you erode.

Climb with me high,
To climatic stature,
Drink me in,
As I am your rapture.

∽ SENSATION ∼

What is this thing?
That floats on the wind,
'Cause I can't get enough,
'Neath grey clouds above.

For it's magic I feel,
And forever I reel,
Amidst within this,
Strange sensation.

When you smile I fly,
Across the blue skies,
A zephyr through my hair,
Caressing me with care.

You remove any foe,
I have on earth below,
I'm forever gliding,
Towards salvation.

When we kiss I expire,
Combusting into fire,
No sense of pain or hurt,
Yet I could almost burst.

Such a delicate taste,
Fires me into space,
Like a rocket of lust,
With passion emblazing.

Amidst passionate love,
From dusk to dusk,
Nothing else matters,
We spill and shatter.

Together as one,
Our senses undone,
We are meant to collide,
Bursting damnation.

I think you are it,
The one & only culprit,
I've never felt this before,
Since you walked through my door.

Now my greatest fear,
Occurs when you're near,
You are my,
Darkest temptation.

⌁ LOVERS LIE ⌁

The sun has become cold as ice,
My love now shunned from your vice,
Tears that trickle down my face,
Mask my emotions of disgrace.

Flooding my lost and desolate soul,
Tossed aside like a broken doll,
As children we would always play,
Gently kissing to fill in our day.

I recall your look into my eyes,
Whenever I yearned between your thighs,
Now it seems that time has past,
Along with our desire and lust.

Shattered worlds now shrink away,
Together you and I no longer sway,
Now that my eyes have become so black,
And the silver moon gently warms my back.

∾ FORBIDDEN KISS ∾

Open your life,
Open your palm,
Let me enter within,
I will do you no harm.

Hold me so tight,
Hold me so close,
As I protect your heart,
From burning sorrow.

Look into my eyes,
Look into my soul,
Basking within your sight,
You make me feel whole.

Whisper gently to me,
Whisper my name,
Absence of words,
Drives me insane.

Touching my skin,
Touching my lips,
Forever I welcome,
Your forbidden kiss.

⌒ JEALOUS RAINBOWS ⌒

I imagine rainbows,
Would be jealous of you,
For having so much beauty,
Hidden in plain view.

You do not need showers,
To come outside and play,
Your beauty is abundant,
Throughout the night and day.

Never needing sunlight,
Glowing in the dark,
With your golden radiance,
Emitting from your heart.

Rainbows may have shoulders,
But they cannot give a hug,
Nor arms to hold and nurture,
The ones you truly love.

Yes rainbows must be jealous,
From their reds to their blues,
Maybe that is why they're crying,
And always following you.

∾ PLEASURE ∾

In the pitch of the night,
From corner of my eye,
A heavenly delight,
She raises a brow.

What shall I do now,
There's only one thing,
I must hear her sing,
In orgasmic,
Ecstasy.

Seated upon leather,
Expecting pleasure,
Seductive bent hips,
Moist luscious lips.

Beckoning my touch,
Seated upon couch,
I must taste her seam,
In sensual,
Pleasure.

∽ JANUARY 2013 ∽

Dear Diary,

I am constantly running out of time to do the things I want. It is so incredibly frustrating as the seemingly trivial matters take a hold of my life and steer me away from my desires. What annoys me more is that I can't quite identify the leading causes and biggest waste of time.

Commuting has to near the top of my list. Hours literally spent every day away from my loved ones travelling to work. I travel for half the hours I work, and then I work more to compensate for lost minutes. This is by no means any form of quality time.

I'm afraid.

I'm afraid that I no longer know what quality time is. My dedication to the job has taken my soul over. I've lost so many years with my loved ones and in the snapshots that I recall, they've all grown so much. In those few moments I've experienced it's been pure magic – just like an illusion.

At least I recognize the problem I guess. Now I just need to fix it through spending more time wi…. no!

INVESTING my time with friends, family, and my closest loved ones.

∾ MOMENTS IN LOVE ⤴

Every ticking moment,
I wish I was there for you,
Every pounding heartbeat,
To show my love so true.

To live every single minute,
As if it was an hour,
Rekindling the love inside,
To a flame that never sours.

I want to harness rainbows,
Deliver them to your hand,
To draw fantasies in the clouds,
Write our names in the wet sand.

Lie down within our orchard,
Upon a bed of fresh grass,
Consuming the fruits of our love,
Where I never wish to fast.

Forever I shall remember,
Holding you ever so tight,
In our moments of despair,
Throughout the darkest nights.

I can't imagine a moment,
This I know is true,
When I never spend a second,
Not thinking about you.

✑ FILTHY FANTASY ✑

Dirty little secrets,
We carefully hide,
With vivacious kisses,
And weakening thighs.

The swirling embrace,
Flooding our mind,
Casting us adrift,
Toward erotic sublime.

With elegant poise,
Our sacred lovers,
Emerge to greet us,
Beneath the covers.

Your eyes widen,
As he comes into view,
Filling you with lust,
Via flesh and sinew.

Craving his touch,
Pleasure with pain,
Yearning to taste,
Milk from his vein.

His hardening body,
Crippling smile,
Your desire to touch,
With the urge to defile.

His beauty,
Overcomes you,
His intention,
Saturates you.

Handing him your mind,
Losing total control,
Prompts you to explore,
Inner depths of your soul.

Letting your digits roam,
As he dam well pleases,
Over your body,
Between the creases.

The thrill of ecstasy,
Across your silky skin,
Trailing your breasts,
Plunging into sin.

Sparks of desire,
Erupt through your core,
Slowly intensifying,
As you drop to the floor.

With your eyes shut,
And body now writhing,
Your fantasy lover,
Becomes so enticing.

So you barely notice,
The latch on the door,
As I enter the room,
You're alone no more…

∿ FALLING ∿

I'm drifting in orbit,
Like space debris,
A celestial object,
Launched by your scream.

Wavering so gently,
My climax resolves,
Trembling in peace,
Together we're whole.

Flowing strong in your bliss,
I'm now falling into you,
Into your sacred earth,
I hope to see it through.

Embrace every long thrust,
As I fall time & time again,
Deep into your love's crust,
Until you say it must end.

With a clap of thunder,
In unison we shall sigh,
My very essence,
Dispersed between your thighs.

Your gravitational pull,
Grasping me with firm hand,
As I continue to fall,
Desecrating sacred land.

Let me be your shooting star,
Falling deep into your sin,
With a gleam in your eye,
As the trembling begins.

My skin stretched so tight,
Pulled taut by your nails,
I can't help but fall,
Once again like hail.

A cataclysmic splashdown,
Your moist soul laps free,
With a rapturous burst,
To wash right over me…

…'til I fall once again.

∂— FREE FALL —∂

A belt of amber embraced the land,
The tarmac of grass upon sand,
As the sun penetrated the horizon,
This jump is just so enticing.

Barely a tweet from any bird,
Lips touch and kiss without a word,
Wheels roll slowly from the hanger,
As the pre-flight check reduces danger.

Heightened danger is a kink today,
Free falling before float and sway,
To skydive together as a tandem,
Anything else would just be random.

Prepared to jump now in the nude,
He's firm, hard, and rather crude,
To embrace the ultimate submission,
She's strapped firmly into position.

The prop whirls…

The engine starts…

His cock spurs…

Her beating heart…

Pistons fueled and are now pumping,
Shadows peel as they were humping,
In tune to his thickening girth,
As they now depart from the earth.

Excitement begins to take her mind,
Thrusting as he fills her from behind,
Propellers whine as they bite,
Sexual ecstasy accompanies the flight.

As he pulls tighter upon the straps,
His entire length between her flaps,
Her body forced tighter into his crutch,
No matter what she could not budge.

Fast approaching ten thousand feet,
Pressure rising within his meat,
Gasping fast for her absent breath,
Veraciously pumping her love nest.

The altimeter peaked…

Her chamber breeched…

Their climax reached…

As she screeched…

Their bodies falling through the air,
Probing her body without a care,
Slowly tumbling head over heals,
Wind compressing their lust seal.

The howling sound across her ears,
Stripped beyond her greatest fear,
As the earth came speeding forth,
Her reverent goddess now poured.

Her heart unable to skip a beat,
His engorged cock within her pleat,
As they tore towards the earth,
While he bore into her purse.

With a rapid but gentle tug,
The shoots deployed high above,
Their bodies slammed with such force,
They climaxed together without remorse.

A surge of pain...

The thrust was insane...

Together they came...

Free falling like rain...

∽ STORM ∽

The grey rubber tires gently purred,
Soaked land swept by grey blue sky,
Anticipation silenced our spoken word,
Pools of lust quelled between your thighs.

Barely a word beyond a single mutter,
"It's just a quiet country drive…"
Suspense caused your heart to flutter,
You could simply tell from my eyes.

My hand slid down as you soaked through,
Fingers teasing with gentle grasp,
Goddess senses my heart is true,
Her gateway now eagerly parts.

You close your eyes, open your heart,
Sensing pleasure and what shall be,
Lost in my motion as we park,
As we gaze out over the sea.

Waves gently crash upon the beach,
Your breath steams as it hits the air,
My fingers sink beyond my reach,
You moan with sensual despair.

Beneath your skirt I plunge in sin,
Your shoulders flex, you heave bosom,
Arching back, I push further in,
Collapsing where you have fallen.

Sea breeze buffers against the car,
The storm sits on the horizon,
Raindrops fall from grey clouds afar,
Gyrating hips are now rising.

Flick of my wrist with the seatbelt,
Unnoticed amidst your pleasure,
Binds you there like rock to sea kelp,
When I tilt the chair to my leisure.

Locked tight and unable to move,
Secured for my own wanton bliss,
Passion, my cock slides in your groove,
Be assured my love, I won't miss.

You can't move,
You're locked in tight,
I anoint your groove,
A lover's plight.

Raindrops now fall,
I plunge into sin,
Up to my balls,
Our lovemaking begins.

I dive deep into your body,
Leaning forward I kiss your lip,
Head rush now making you groggy,
Your lifeblood swirls within your hips.

Lost expression upon your face,
Fucking you deeper and harder,
Forcing your body to my pace,
Our heaving bodies thrust faster.

The storm breaks through thunder above,
With a boom shattering our souls,
Sordid passion scorches our love,
Together we are complete and whole.

Surrounded by Mother Nature,
As she ruptures with icy hail,
You embrace my pulsating girth,
Like a slave embraces the flail.

The brink of orgasmic pleasure,
Now lies so close within your reach,
Clenching to my sunken treasure,
Thunderous waves pounding the beach.

A force so mighty it's frightening,
Heavy thunder and lightening cracks,
My essence pours, it's enlightening,
Ecstatic current rips through your back.

Mother Nature's tears start falling,
Orchestral patter of her rain,
Our tantric souls are left souring,
As your body hugs my love vein.

The storm overhead passes by,
Sweeping clean the salty sea air,
We collapse and release a sigh,
Your fingers running through my hair.

∾ IN MY GIMP ⟿

The mist rising within,
Upon the surge of my breath,
Creeping like human sin,
Within the mask on my head.

A gentle frost,
As I settle my heart,
My mind becomes lost,
As she tears me apart.

My lady in black,
Leather and lace,
Her whip cuts no slack,
As it sears my face.

Splitting my white flesh,
From chin to my mouth,
Ensures sting of the best,
When my sweat pours south.

Her words command me to last,
My head hanging in shame,
Throb of her whip on my arse,
For tonight, I have no name.

As the blood mingles in,
With sweat from my brow,
I'm roasting hot within,
This suit made from a cow.

Cocooned in black leather,
Rubber and steel,
Forced to her whither,
Through pain we both feel.

Cries are then stopped,
By my cherry red gimp,
Flesh tarnished by her crop,
Pink as a boiled shrimp.

I'm about to expire,
Lack of fill in my lung,
She doesn't let me retire,
This is way too much fun.

She feeds me some air,
So that I may then fight,
I know she cares,
Despite a throttle so tight.

Cupped around my throat,
Eyes beginning to bulge,
Drenched and soaked,
Prepped for my cuckold.

Beginning to drift,
Now floating through time,
To her I submit,
To enter the sublime.

I am hers as she likes,
On my hands, on my knees,
In my gimp I delight,
In my gimp I believe.

∞ UNCHAIN YOUR MIND ∞

It waits for your soul,
Beyond any horizon,
Like a bottomless hole,
With such immense tension.

It's there for the taking,
As sand sifts on a beach,
Passionate forsaken,
Falling through your reach.

It's my love and passion,
Scorching with lust,
It's nothing you could imagine,
A gravitational thrust.

There's no visible limits,
Beyond blue skies above,
Turning hours into minutes,
My somewhat endless love.

No shadows are cast,
Nor footsteps taken,
Gentle kisses will last,
As senses are stolen.

Come enter my arms,
Make me your destiny,
Protector of harm,
Purveyor of ecstasy.

Take hold of my hand,
You shall feel how I'm kind,
Journey with me to the land,
Where I'll unchain your mind.

❧ RESURRECTION ☙

Simmering heat,
Upon the horizon,
A musical beat,
To slowly rise upon.

Rays of sunshine,
Cut through the dark,
Like rhythm and rhyme,
From an echoing harp.

Our bodies ache,
Aftermath of our fast,
Within a tantric wake,
Of climaxing past.

Gasping for breath,
Air scented with musk,
Our bodies transcend,
Collapsing like dust.

A tear from your eye,
Mixed with lusts sweat,
An orgasmic writhe,
Our desire is now whet.

Trembling and shaking,
Straddled between thighs,
I rise like the king,
As the sun greets the sky.

The still aching pond,
From goddesses thirst,
Ripples as my frond,
Hardens within your purse.

She shudders and quakes,
Heart falls to the floor,
Your body I forsake,
As I rise for more.

Plunging into the depth,
Of goddesses chamber,
A dry gasp of breath,
Ignites my ember.

Trawling within,
With strokes so kind,
Souls bathing in sin,
A departure of mind.

You're no longer there,
I thrust and you sway,
Silent scream in despair,
Floods the new day.

She clenches so tight,
I dispel my erection,
Opening your eyes,
To my tantric resurrection.

∾ MAKE ME ∾

A cafe outing,
Short skirt with no panties,
Oak table,
With rose.

She teases me with her toes,
Seductively rubbing
The tension,
Grows.

Together we depart,
Hailing a cab,
Caressing,
My trousered length.

The driver's eyes diverting,
Just out of sight,
'Till I'm almost,
Spent.

Finally we arrive home,
I open the door,
She grabs,
My tie.

Passionately she then reaches,
Grasping my hair,
I'm forced,
Between thigh.

Amidst our lust frenzy,
We then stumble,
Before falling,
Upon the stairs.

Forcing my hand to comfort,
Beneath her skirt,
Gently,
She unfolds.

Her delicate lips moistened,
Wrapped around my knuckle,
Before she,
Surrounds my wrist.

She cries with unbridled passion,
With aching song pleasure,
Vigorously,
Unleashing me.

Her muffled moans leak,
Resonating deep,
Around my,
Unleashed girth.

Rolling upon her back,
Shoulders upon the steps,
Her thighs,
Restrict me.

I plunge my steady length,
Deep within,
Her surging,
Bliss.

My hips bear down,
Her grasp tightens,
Her moans,
Silently trickle.

Bonded within her,
My erection throbbing,
I pry,
We climb.

Step by step we rise,
Fucking her hard,
Scaling,
The stairs upward.

Her poor aching buttocks,
Spanked by every step,
Bruised and battered,
Red.

At the summit of the stair,
Fingers entangled in my hair,
We rise,
Bonded together.

I whip off my leather belt,
Together with my tie,
I bind her,
To open thigh.

Ankles bound to each,
Stairwell rail,
She's breeched,
Suspended.

I watch her struggle,
To compose herself,
Positioning,
Only for me.

Slowly I enter her,
Again,
And again,
And again.

Exhaustion never betrays,
Her body holds firm,
As I plunge,
Into her fiery depth.

My vantage point,
Her polished mound,
I press,
A finger into her.

Vigorously plunging,
Tenaciously rubbing,
Trembling upon the wake,
Of her own waves.

As she gushes,
Again,
And again,
And again.

Completely broken,
I unbind her,
She collapses,
Into my arms.

Resting upon breath,
She snuggles into me,
Trembling,
With after shocks.

Like a feather I carry her,
To rest upon our bed?
No.
To make love once again.

PJ BAYLISS

❧ FEBRUARY 2013 ❧

Dear Diary,

For the want of a gift for those I love, however, I have empty pockets once again. I could blame the dentist, bank, mechanic, and accountant, but ultimately I blame myself. I blame myself for my own inadequacies and failings, which is completely crazy.

It is such a pleasure to give. I crave it, hunger it, and can't help myself to provide. I'm a people pleaser, prepared to become bankrupt in order to satisfy my own selfless desires.

Chocolates may be cheaper than diamonds, but they say the gift of love is priceless. Love is one thing I cannot buy after all, nor can I pawn it for gifts from the store. Somehow I must gift my love without emptying my pockets.

Just what is a "gift of love"?

Gifting love is the trick, I guess. I just want to gift the one thing nobody could ever own – my soul and myself.

ᴔ— GIFTED —ᴔ

He lies there upon white linen sheets,
She curiously opens her eye,
His masculine chest, throat, chin exposed,
She tenderly slips over his thigh.

His deep sleep cascades into slumber,
His morning vein feels so bliss,
Softly she trickles her body over
Like an early morning mist.

Carefully she maneuvers,
Sliding his firmness inside,
His shallow dream now dissolving,
She grasps his throat as a guide.

She hovers lower against him,
Every surface of skin pressed hard,
She rocks gentle to settle him,
As she massages his erect shaft.

Rhythmically she displaces,
Her hips grind against his waist,
She rises toward the heavens,
Gyrating to fill every space.

Her hands reaching for his body,
Grappling his rippling chest,
Deepening breaths of lust exhale,
Together they emit such a sweet zest.

With a sudden urge to break,
Her lover wakes up from his dream,
Realizing his hidden desire,
Firmly wedged within her seam.

His bulging member lodged firmly,
Her fingers stroking his muscular thighs,
Now so close, she begins to render,
His hands strike between her cries.

A torrent of lust and passion,
She firmly grasps her breasts,
Oozes reverently in sacrifice,
Before silently holding in her breath.

His silky flesh of amber,
Erupts thick creamy seed when shifted,
She asks if he liked her parcel,
He says, "You're beautifully gifted."

∽ PRECIOUS P's PARCEL ∾

Oh my beautiful subject,
The lovely Precious P,
You taught me to roll,
Look what you've done to me.

Left over right,
Right over left,
Pulling the ends tight,
Restrains your head.

One golden buckle,
Black leather strap,
A studded collar,
Surrounds your neck.

A slither of silver,
Stainless steel bar,
Strapped to your ankles,
Spreads your thighs far.

Patiently waiting,
Or perhaps through no choice,
Waiting the command,
From my deep voice.

The deathly silence,
Nothing dares stirs,
A flick of a switch,
Machinery whirs.

Translucent gel,
Smeared on your crust,
The cold hardened steel,
Enters with a thrust.

Gasp of your breath,
A bountiful sigh,
Whimsical tear,
Escapes your eye.

PJ BAYLISS

A drop from your cheek,
Approaches the floor,
I prop open your mouth,
To fill in your jaw.

Those voluptuous lips,
So tight like a clam,
The rasp of your teeth,
Surrounding my glans.

Locks of your hair,
My fingers entwined,
Connect like the ocean,
When I paddle your hind.

You squirm with the sting,
But dare not clench,
My hips roll in desire,
Riding my loved wench.

For squirming I punish,
No matter how much,
I affix to your collar,
A gorgeous butt plug.

Gazing down at my girth,
Your exquisite eyes,
Steady & transfixed,
Yet trembling thighs.

You hear me growl,
While suckling my root,
Don't let me spill,
Upon my Armani suit.

Without missing a beat,
Or moment to spare,
My partner in crime,
Fills you in where he dares.

A pop of the plug,
Short simmer of pain,
Replaced with his snug,
Cock riddled with veins.

He lathers you up,
As the machine plunges down,
And I thrust as you gulp,
Gazing up at my frown.

Filled to the brink,
In your every corner,
Ready to come,
When I shall order.

His seed spilling forth,
Down your silk thigh,
You know it's now right,
As you look in my eye.

My taste permeates,
Then my fingers relax,
You gorge upon me,
Without pulling back.

Our bodies climax,
With such sexual rigor,
Oozing with lust,
Bathing in it's glimmer.

I reach down to release,
The saturated knots,
Thank you Precious P,
How you've shown me a lot.

∿ CAPTIVATED ∿

You said you would never,
Forget the day we sighed,
That moment you captured me,
With your ice blue eyes.

I remember it so clearly,
Trembling feet upon doormat,
Those innocent schoolgirl lips,
Long dark brown in a plat.

We loved that summer together,
Relaxing upon the beach,
I reveled within your beauty,
Like a golden sun-kissed peach.

You offered me sanctuary,
Sealed upon our first kiss,
I provided you my soul,
Our love, I thought, was bliss.

We promised ourselves forever,
Something I thought would last,
But I recall that night,
Those black clouds floated past.

You pulled my heart to pieces,
Tore it clear in half,
That night you left me standing,
As you walked your own path.

Tears filled up my shadow,
Till not one drop was left,
Tears that still whelm up,
That summer was the best.

I'll know you kept your promise,
When you read this verse & sigh,
I will always remain your captive,
Beneath this pond within my eyes.

✌ VALEN-UNTIE ME ✌

Within a shadow of flickering flame,
Pulsating surge of passionate vein,
Anointed by kiss from delicate lips,
Destined to penetrate sin between hips.

Darkness shrouds my innocent eyes,
Tongue travelling length of my thigh,
Essence of lust driving me insane,
Waiting your touch where I'm fain.

Sensual whispers into my ear,
Awakens me to a new fear,
Frozen still as you command,
Embracing the sting from your hand.

Flashes of white surrounding red,
Trepidation drifting within my head,
Threshold of pain teased by your palm,
You leave me pain but deliver no harm.

Silk scarf now saturated with tears,
Genteel numbness across my rear,
Skin scorched with desire so gently,
Submitted as you now untie me.

◦— THE BOX —◦

Whispers of sunlight herald in the new day,
Jostling shadows retreat as they play,
Sublime submission of the dim light,
Lovers arise after tears spilled overnight.

Icy and stray dark soul wonders by,
Etched & scarred through emotional lies,
Passion bleeds through orifice of lust,
Tear drops causing flesh hinges to rust.

Love filled rapture tops everyone's list,
Obscured due to lost love's rich mist,
Lying alongside one yet calling another,
Accused are flayed by their inert lovers.

My black box is opened and now filling,
Confessions and praise from the willing,
Playful images of wanton lovers who play,
Transforms into dreams towards end of day.

One thing at a time now I keep saying,
Cruel hands of the clock keep swaying,
Demons compel this task to be done,
As I retreat to my box under the sun.

I realize this lost journey's a mystery,
Baffling, contentious, yet it torments me,
Irresistible sensual desire seems right,
Forcing me from the black into the white.

✍ THE CURE ✍

Feeling poorly and torn,
I rise before the dawn,
Dry as dust with my thirst,
With my lust about to burst.

Despite holding a fever,
My flesh remains eager,
So I have a little think,
And call in Nurse Kink.

She arrived in black heels,
Skirt that barely concealed,
Her gorgeous bare thighs,
Such an object of desire.

From the foot of my bed,
She sensed that my head,
Was flooded with blood,
Hard 'n' ready for love.

With her tender touch,
She proceeded to wash,
My hips flexed and lunged,
Under her wet sponge.

Her smile turned to smirk,
As she continued to work,
Now aware of my bliss,
She called for an assist.

From across the dim ward,
Heels clicked upon the floor,
Frames so delicate and tender,
Only an artist could render.

PJ BAYLISS

They controlled my urge to resist,
Binding tight my twitching wrist,
Prepping me for a journey,
On that stainless steel gurney.

That sponge deep in my lap,
Opposed any attempt to relax,
As I writhed and then heaved,
They bound and tied my feet.

Now fixed by all four limbs,
I was incarcerated by sin,
Which only became worse,
At the will of these nurses.

With my wrists tied to the bed,
Unable to move as such,
No choice but to submit,
To Nurse Kink and her clit.

She straddled my trussed hand,
To embrace her moist land,
As my face became smothered,
By one of the others.

My spare hand was filled,
By a nurse poised to spill,
Who vigorously bucked,
By this kinky hand fuck.

As my body was shared,
My feet were not spared,
I was massaged, as such,
By a tight, shaven crotch.

Nurses were a plenty,
Within a sexual frenzy,
Thrusting and sucking,
In a pile of wild fucking.

The gurney strained and groaned,
As I became totally owned,
While a nurse raised her frock,
To consume my erect cock.

Beyond my wildest dreams,
I was consumed by their seams,
With an earth trembling shatter,
Saturating me in their splatter.

I was so lost in this mess,
But still stuck in her nest,
Which continued to thrust,
Till I was ready to bust.

Locked in and bound tight,
Unable to move or writhe,
Yet I trembled, then burst,
With an all-mighty spurt.

As my creamy seed streamed,
Nurse Kink quietly beamed,
Taking pleasure at my lunge,
As she wiped me with her sponge.

At rest upon my rest bed,
With swollen and inert head,
Now cured of my hot fever,
Through this course of hot beaver.

"My dear, Here's your little pill"
Said Nurse Kink with a thrill,
Before my mind slipped away,
Bringing night to my day.

∾ I FEEL ∾

I feel you watching me,
From a distance so great,
I slip under the cover,
Beckoning my fate.

I feel your eyes upon me,
Glowing warm like the sun,
Consuming my flesh,
Envisioning us as one.

I feel your breath surround me,
Trickling down my neck,
Like a glacier of fire,
En route to certain wreck.

I feel the silken cloth,
Binding sight from my eyes,
When you tie the knot,
My soul melts in desire.

I feel your hot tongue,
Trawling across my skin,
Tasting my perfumed scent,
Beckoning me to sin.

I feel a gentle pinch,
Squeezing fingertips,
Nerves gather in delight,
Awaiting crack of whip.

I feel the air snap,
Breaking as you crack,
Just before the singe,
Red welts upon my back.

I feel your energy rise,
Like the resurrection,
My hunger for you inside,
To feast upon your erection.

I feel your soul upon me,
Resting upon my lip,
Trembling with my thirst,
I consume your mushroomed tip.

I feel you upon the taste bud,
Bed within my mouth,
Now drizzling with moisture,
From regions further south.

I feel your fingers entwine,
Through my long hair,
Grasping and pulling me in,
Towards you with such care.

I feel a sudden pop,
From buttons on my shirt,
As you tear it from my body,
To fuck me 'till it hurts.

I feel your firm hand,
An endeavor not to come,
As you caress my goddess,
Glove me with your thumb.

I feel you in the darkness,
From deep inside and out,
Biting my bottom lip,
To silence any shout.

I feel my tide turning,
Steaming inside so hot,
You're my surge in the ocean,
Making waves with your cock.

I feel the cresting mountains,
Of turbulent waters inside,
Struggling to compose,
From rapture between my thighs.

I feel your every inch,
Impaling my burning soul,
I've never felt so lost,
As you plunder my sacred hole.

I feel you whisper now,
Your permission is given,
I pour myself upon you,
And we bathe in our sin.

∾ MARCH 2013 ∾

Dear Diary,

This "passion" always existed among us. It has coursed through the veins of our ancestors for centuries from the dawn of time. Like a deep limestone spring, it has slowly permeated through society and now flows upon the plains of society, out into the open.

Naturally, I was going to be swept away. Social media ensured the flood came quickly and from all directions while my thirst for passion compelled me to wade into the waters. Like the many others, I was invigorated by the spring waters as if the drought of mankind was finally broken.

Passion has always been there, only it was hidden. The Rock 'n' Roll era helped to break down the dam that prevented it from flowing. Now, the waters surround us and promises to sweep our souls away.

I want to swim in the depths of passion and desire. To have it touch my skin and infiltrate my soul. I want the inevitable to come and wash me away.

✦ MY MISTAKE ✦

I should have known better,
Oh my god how I tried,
To love and to serve you,
Until the day I die.

I know I should've listened,
And I should have complied,
Will you ever understand,
Just how hard I did try.

But know I really know,
How hard it is to love,
One another when,
Push comes to shove.

My mistake has now past,
Both our lives are torn,
As we walk life's path,
So battered and worn.

I wish I had forgotten,
My distant past,
I should have remembered,
I belong in your heart.

∽ THE BROKEN SOUL MYSTERY ∾

The smoke filled the room,
As she walked on by,
I felt swept by a broom,
As I gazed at her thigh.

My heart started to swoon,
Noticing a tear from her eye,
So I took her hand,
To comfort her as a man.

Her life was torn apart,
By her stilted lover,
Love was now a mere laugh,
Especially under the covers.

A possible affair of the heart,
Had taken her significant other,
As I wiped her tear,
She smiled so sincere.

That smile hit my flank,
As I gasped and sighed,
My mind was now outranked,
By feeling between my thighs.

My heart certainly sank,
As she ceased to cry,
Her hand broke free,
And trawled over me.

Her touch felt like satin,
Finger nails like pretty jewels,
Compelling me to action,
Igniting my sensual fuel.

I wanted this broken vixen,
To fix her with my tool,
This moment was bliss,
We sealed it with a kiss.

We touched soul to soul,
And solved the mystery,
Of her hearts dark hole,
And where her love be.

That evening we then strolled,
As she voiced her plea,
Take my pain away,
And I'll love you everyday.

⌁ SACRIFICE MY LOVE ⌁

How I wish that I was blind,
So that I may then ignore,
The countless many crimes,
Fallen souls on distant shores.

They sacrifice their souls,
Taking innocent lives,
Separating the men,
From children and their wives.

From this I cannot hide,
Nor shelter those I love,
Yet I will not deny,

With passion they prevail,
Freedom their only goal,
To take another life,

Tragedy compels me,
To sacrifice my love,
Place my hatred aside,
Resign myself to lust.

I must find my escape,
From this dark burnt world,
To feel the warmth emerge,
From the arms of my girl.

❧ THE VALEDICTION CEREMONY ☙

A veil of silence trickles across the floor,
Dusty slither of light projects from the door,
Her shadow creeps softly out from toe,
Awaiting her lover of friend and foe.

Slithering light snaps open into space,
Painted innocence sits upon her face,
As lusts silhouette is launched in the air,
His essence of musk lingers with despair.

Cold distilled atmosphere is sliced apart,
From tension of warmth within his heart,
Her spirit compelled towards submission,
Body composed for his lusts commission.

His thick fingers gloved with black leather,
Grasping coiled rope to which he'll tether,
Her wrists, elbows, ankles and then thighs,
Ensuring his wicked passage of love inside.

A solemn eye inspecting the delicate lace,
Adorning her body basking in pure faith,
Her once trembling heart beating so calm,
At peaceful ease without fear of any harm.

His muscular thighs, arms, and rippled torso,
So capable of blemishing marks of Bordeaux,
Her mind once shrouded in darkness is freed,
She vows her soul shall meet his every need.

His deep-seated voice requests for permission,
To love like no other through her submission,
Her reply comes as a song of divine clement,
I beg to remain, Sir…
…Your most humble and obedient servant.

∽ LOST BRIDE ∽

She walks in beauty throughout the night,
Trawling her lost soul behind her,
A bride of desire shadowed by light,
Destined to become fate's lover.

Delicate flower held with her palm,
A white veil covering her eye,
Beating heart exposes inner calm,
Blue satin and lace adorns her thigh.

Her face decorated like a china doll,
Lips glowing deep red with lust,
Slowly she marches to offer her soul,
Towards her lover scented in musk.

Her father gifts her hand upon arm,
Practically molded from his own clay,
Tear from his eye ensure there is no harm,
As she departs from his house today.

White veil is lifted upon the breeze,
As flowers sway gently in the wild,
A kiss silently brings her soul to ease,
The lost bride is no longer a child.

∾ I GIVE IN ∾

A flick of a switch,
Darkness penetrates,
Upon sight of my twitch,
Beauty illuminates.

Your flesh soft as sand,
Near buried treasure,
Buckling under my hand,
Besotted in pleasure.

Precious beauty so vain,
My sleeping princess,
Until you revel in pain,
When goddess flinches.

Eyes gazing in hope,
Biting bottom lip,
Thighs stretched by rope,
Searing your hips.

Wrists cuffed and spread,
Sacrificed you splay,
Teased with my head,
I own you today.

Eyes whiten with fear,
Bright as the moon,
Sliding into your rear,
Threatening monsoon.

You shudder in my wake,
Of sensation play,
Spanked till you flake,
Don't come 'till I say.

Stretched like a winch,
Frozen in time,
A curl from my twitch,
Your pain is mine.

Nerves scattering away,
A retreating tide,
Soul flooded with dismay,
As I spank your hide.

A moan is set free,
From clinched jaw,
Digging into you, ecstasy,
My hardened claw.

Suffering until numb,
My desire permeates,
Thrusting we are one,
Recklessly we fornicate.

Wave cresting as I stroke,
Delicate as pure silk,
Resigned amidst lost hope,
I feed you my lust milk.

Sweat drenches your eyes,
Horizons are blurred,
Gimp silences your sighs,
Truly shaken, not stirred.

Plundering your depth,
Craving release,
Swept in my vortex,
Immobilized by my beast.

I draw out my blade,
Slicing the rope,
Your soul cascades,
Flooding me as I stroke.

You pleased me my pet,
Drenched in our sin,
For you never said,
I want to give in.

PJ BAYLISS

∂ ORGY ∂

It was just a simple invite,
Headlined: "Come as you are",
And they arrived in hoards,
From near and from afar.

To revel within each other,
Feasting upon naked flesh,
Exploring our sinful pleasures,
Bodies entwining like mesh.

My fingers glancing over,
The hardened shaft and knob,
As I opened the door,
With my loving heart-throb.

A hand there to greet us,
With a eager smile or two,
The atmosphere ecstatic,
In that room with no view.

As a finger ran across,
My subtle, pouting lip,
A hand upon my waist,
Settling firmly on my hip.

My nerves went to market,
Scattering each which way,
When I sighted the black leather,
Hammock for which to sway.

Just then my shirt revealed,
My erect nipples underneath,
When one of my suitors,
Gently caressed my seam.

With a firm and mighty yank,
My buttons popping off,
Exposing me to them all,
My skin, fresh & soft.

My heart-throb was ignited,
Of this I had no doubt,
From the smile now in place,
Where once there was a pout.

With a flick from a wrist,
Upon my buttoned jean,
They fell toward the ground,
Revealing my thighs so lean.

As my heart-throb sighted,
My excitement, plain to see,
I was culprit to his need,
Kneeling right before me.

Fingers running through his hair,
As he firmly palmed my hips,
A lump grew within his throat,
As he surrounded me with his lips.

His tongue explored my girth,
While my parched lips moaned,
He left me wanting much more,
He left me cleansed and honed.

When my vision had returned,
Heart-throb stood before me,
Gently smiling in satisfaction,
She was as naked as can be.

Her nipples were bright red,
Standing hard upon the edge,
Feet were partially parted,
Like a submissive pledge.

His attention turned to her,
To satisfy her every need,
She shuddered as his tongue,
Flicked across goddess's seed.

Together we now caressed her,
She stood there quiet and still,
Whispering "You are my guy,
You are my sensual thrill."

Her throat arching backward,
Famished taste buds dining,
I caressed her soft bosom,
His tongue flicked her lining.

She crumpled like paper,
Within my tight embrace,
I shall never forget,
The delight upon her face.

He looked up at me,
Suggested we should swap,
I watched him penetrate,
Her mouth with his cock.

As another appeared,
From over my shoulder,
With a gristly hard shaft,
Shaven balls like boulders.

Heart-throb then grasped,
The cock of yet another,
Gasping between thrusts,
"Fuck me please, my lover."

My erection now flooded,
Surging with love seed,
I wrapped my swollen member,
In a string of pearl beads.

With her eyesight hindered,
By his thrusting torso,
I slipped myself in,
To her swirling Bordeaux.

She convulsed as I plunged,
My throbbing hot tip,
In between her thighs,
Narrowly missing her clit.

Each row of white bead,
Rattling her chamber,
Through her pleasure zone,
With my meaty savor.

When a choking gasp,
Emerged from my lover,
I knew he wasn't done,
It was time for yet another.

Within her grasping hot hand,
Was a member now freed,
Steamy and pulsating,
Drooling with thick seed.

I wiped off her chin,
Continued my flurry,
Raking all the walls,
Of my heart-throb's quarry.

I bore through her flesh,
Before she recovered,
Writhing in her husk,
My exhausted lover.

A gleam in her eye,
I misread it as love,
As a behemoth of a man,
From behind me did shove.

I was caught right off-guard,
They say love is blind,
Yet he gently wore me,
Like a glove from behind.

I was sandwiched now,
Like meat in between butter,
Such a curious feeling,
Bringing me to stutter.

The pair of us working,
Her into a frenzy,
My decorated girth,
Filling her up plenty.

Three bodies clashing,
Colliding with force,
Peering over her forehead,
Was a cock like a horse.

Her neck arching up,
As he thumbed back her chin,
Extruding his entire length,
To where her chest begins.

Right before my eyes,
I revealed in the sight,
The speed of his thrust,
Motion of his might.

My beast from behind,
Convulsed insanely,
Dormant we lay,
Inside her resonating.

What felt like minutes,
Turned closer to hours,
Leaving my heart-throb soaking,
From numerous lust showers.

Her bounty replenished,
She placed me down,
Upon my aching back,
Where she went to town.

My pearl bead necklace,
Preventing me thus far,
From ejaculating,
I was near, yet so far.

Her tongue danced politely,
Upon my numb tip,
Before she consumed,
Me inside her love pit.

My depth within was perfect,
But not a perfect fit,
Every single movement,
Gave such a subtle grit.

Our bodies writhing,
Like serpents embroiled in sin,
Colliding with such passion,
Embracing the conflict within.

Tension grasped my lover,
Her moment had arrived,
Baring down her hips,
Spine arching toward the sky.

My pressure rising,
For my rodeo girl,
Hollering my name,
Lost within a twirl.

My precious lover,
Collapsed in a heap,
Triggering my release,
By pulling the beads.

My essence pouring,
Upon my navel,
I cried with desire,
To move, I was unable.

Never ever before,
And never since,
Have the pair of us loved,
Till we no longer can clinch.

✌ A DISTANT PLEASURE ✌

Lying there quietly in the blue,
So detached from myself,
While waiting for you,
To come and bed her.

Her nervous pulse echoing,
Rapid heart beat,
Blood pulsating,
While completely motionless.

Slowly she rose to her feet,
While I watched,
From my seat,
Hidden from view.

Admiring her curvaceous hips,
Glossy red cherry line,
Upon her soft lips,
She was simply perfect.

Then a click of the door,
As he entered,
And crossed the floor,
To our burning desire.

I watched her turn her back,
As he prepared,
The things to whack,
Her creamy complexion.

My lips dried and cracked,
As my hot breath,
Escaped the gap,
Atop of my quivering tongue.

PJ BAYLISS

His hand he then offered,
For her to firmly take,
Before she then hovered,
To his side.

With a flick of his thumb,
He lowered her pants,
Revealing her buttocks,
And her perfect stance.

Without a spoken word,
He laid her down,
Like a wounded bird,
Wings spread wide open.

Carefully his hand strokes,
As she shuddered,
In lost hope,
For her spanking.

The thick tension in the air,
Snapped with a flash,
When he struck her bare,
Delicate flesh.

I flinched at the sound,
While I watched,
From my hidden ground,
At her punishment.

When she yelped at his touch,
He somehow knew,
It wasn't too much,
For her to handle.

She was now just lying there,
Plump and so limp,
With a single tear,
Falling from her cheek.

It was time for him to leave,
Passing her on,
To my company,
For our own pleasure.

As he shut the wooden door,
I then approached,
Her for remorse,
And sultry love making.

Tenderly I caressed,
Her aching wounds,
And heaving breast,
Of my dearest angel.

I knew she still felt the pain,
Yet the remedy,
Was just a plain,
Kiss from my lips.

I placed my thumb upon her chin,
As our lips touched,
Our tongues flicked in,
Each other's nectar.

I held her close within my arms,
Amidst my warmth,
Away from harm,
With all of my love.

♪ PURITY ♪

A twist of a bolt,
Coupled, sudden jolt,
My subject was taut,
Chained tight to my fort.

Lines from each post,
To the limbs of my host,
Stretched her out to points,
Slowly, I anoint.

Oil, scented lotion,
Circular motion,
Drips from cap,
O'er neck, breasts, lap.

With a whimpering cry,
I anoint her thighs,
Begging for passage,
As I gently massaged.

My fingers & palm,
Rubbed in the balm,
Sinew and muscle,
Every inch of my morsel.

She groaned, writhed.
As I crossed her inner thigh,
I could perceive how,
She wanted me now.

For she twinkled like a star,
At the gateway to her path,
Glistening wet,
Delicate pet.

So I sunk the tip,
Of my tongue in her pit,
The chains barely chattered,
As her courage gathered.

As I buried in so deep,
She slowly began to weep,
Bursting open like a flower,
In a soft souring shower.

I had to stop and admire,
Goddesses fire,
It beckoned me,
To set her lust free.

Rolling through the flesh,
Of my captive pledge,
Which I did in delight,
Like a moon chasing night.

Blood pumped through my fare,
Rising high in the air,
She let loose a stutter,
Parting like soft butter.

Her voice lost upon breath,
I inserted my length,
Unable to writhe,
For how she was tied.

Stretched limb to limb,
For the purpose of my sin,
To explore every gap,
From my head to my sack.

PJ BAYLISS

Filling her compact,
As she lay upon back,
From her throat, a moan,
I hit her pleasure zone.

Again and once again,
Like a meaty boomerang,
Muscles began to cramp,
Intense pain as I spanked.

Releasing an amber shower,
From passions' raw power,
As her toes unfurled,
Entering my world.

Where pain embraced,
Mists of subspace,
The shallows of her mind,
While I orchestrated time.

Through a steady beat,
With my baton of meat,
In tune to her heart,
Pumping so fast.

Now everything clenched,
Even her teeth clenched,
As her waters ripped free,
And gently anoint me.

For a moment I rest,
Deep within her nest,
Revelling in her seep,
Then, a little creep.

Just when her lust wave,
Crested where splayed,
Left with little choice,
A screech from her voice.

An orgasmic repent,
Extremely sensitive,
And how this did show,
From her flushed afterglow.

As her lungs collapsed,
I repeated my lap,
Again and then again,
My mighty meat engine.

Pistons were pumping,
To her shackled humping,
Abandoned, without care,
Our salty mists stung the air.

Till finally she was numb,
Her safe-word then rung,
Ears ringing in silence,
Her breathless relent.

I removed my lust beast,
Her taught straps, I released,
Shackles taken in,
Basking in our sin.

From her aching love purse,
She drifted back to earth,
Returning back to me,
In a pool of purity.

∾ KINKY LOVE ∾

Shuffling so nervously,
In her skirt with ironed pleats,
Knee-high leather boots,
I approached her in my suit.

We met there in the Autumn sun,
As our lips melted to become one,
Although no one spoke a word,
Her burning soul was clearly heard.

Her fingers slipped into mine,
They felt so silky and divine,
We strolled along the path,
Connecting heart to heart.

Ours was such a special love,
Without a push but with a shove,
As Autumn leaves embraced dusk,
Our bodies filled with raw hot lust.

In a sheltered glen within the park,
As shadows welcomed in the dark,
I now untied her long flowing hair,
Binding her wrists so petite and bare.

With my belt I secured her foot,
Around a trunk I then took,
The leather strap around the trunk,
I could hear her heart go thump.

I didn't care what others saw,
My desire had no remorse,
My lover had no ounce of hope,
As from my bag I pulled a rope.

She gasped with a sudden shock,
Before I tied a firm reef knot,
Wrapping it around her chest,
Restraining her heaving breast.

PJ BAYLISS

Bound tight with no place to go,
While her goddess gently flowed,
My hands worked her every inch,
Until she felt the cold steel pinch.

A clamp upon her hard erect,
Nipple with such a sensual effect,
As she surrendered herself willfully,
Before writhing in devilish glee.

While my leather belt held her legs,
Apart so wide and ideal for pegs,
To be attached to her tingling flesh,
To the delight of my kinky pledge.

Secured and bound to the tree,
My lover gazed up to me,
As I sunk my fingers in,
Deep into her pulsing sin.

She murmured under the pain,
As I released my love vein,
Pressing it between her thighs,
Inserting myself deep as she sighed.

Grinding my torso with firm force,
As our bodies found their own course,
My soul slowly seeping within,
Filling her full to the brim.

With my release I suddenly thrust,
Deeper inside her moist crust,
Sending the taut pegs free,
As she cried out in ecstasy.

That sudden release of pain,
Sent her streaming like rain,
Pouring her inner soul out,
With an orgasmic pout.

∾ A SPANKING A DAY ∾

Relax my baby doll,
Can you not see?
This spanking hurts,
You more than me.

Do not weep my love,
Try not to cry,
As I whip off my belt,
With a deep solemn sigh.

Take care my child,
Embrace this pain,
As I gift it with love,
To honor your shame.

As my own Mother once said,
To my face as her child,
That a good spanking a day,
Will ensure I am not wild.

Her tenderness I wore,
In the form of red welts,
Her message was carried,
By Father's trusty leather belt.

PJ BAYLISS

I could not understand this,
Old fashioned discipline,
As it tore away at my hide,
Ripping through my innocence.

Yet for you my baby doll,
Should you happen to think,
My swift steady motion,
Is nothing else but our kink.

Pain brings us down,
When we're flying high,
Reminding us,
Of the reason why.

Something I must offer,
To reflect our deep love,
Be sure not to stutter,
When enough is enough.

In a world full of anguish,
Terror, hate and pain,
Tears serve to remind us,
Life will never wane.

∾ DREAMSCAPE ∾

I hover dawn to dusk,
Dreaming of your touch,
Your absence leaves me forlorn,
Does my request for love seem too much?

The cool night air surrounds me,
I close my desolate eyes,
My lost mind is set free,
Rapidly flooding with desire.

Immersed within my emotion,
Drunk from the summer wine,
As you bow down before me,
Your silky hair now entwined.

I lift your soul from the earth,
Fingers holstered on your chin,
My lips seal with passionate kiss,
You body quivers with expectant sin.

Embrace the black silk cloth,
As I firmly tighten the knot,
Let my darkness filter through,
For my light shall not stop.

Trembling there before me,
In silence you wait and hope,
A gathering of your wrists,
I bind them tight with rope.

Sensual pressure that burns,
From the perfumed hemp,
Your heart beats and blood churns,
Mixing sweat into the scent.

A pouting lip beneath the mask,
Tempting me to enter within,
My firmness fills your mouth,
You gasp breathless in sin.

Such a delicate touch,
Rasping me with your teeth,
Flooded lust heading south,
My soul simmering beneath.

The sense of your wet tongue,
Darting over my shaft,
Tempting me to come,
Ensuring I am rock hard.

Withdrawal from your kiss,
A tug upon your lead,
My target is your bliss,
Intent to release my seed.

A firm but gentle hand,
Sprawls you upon the bed,
I sight my promised land,
And slowly insert my aching head.

Sliding further within,
Your gasps suggest I should stop,
Soaked through in your sin,
Down comes my riding crop.

A stripe across your arse,
Searing pain sent up your spine,
My touch that shall now last,
Like the finish of aged wine.

Clenched tight you bear the mark,
Absorbing the heat from red stripe,
Your lost mind soon departs,
As I pump until you are ripe.

My thrusts are firm and fast,
Your soft eyes start to dilate,
Suddenly you now clasp,
As I insert a device that vibrates.

Intoxicated by this pleasure,
Twisted by device and flesh,
Your balance tilted by my measure,
I sense you're close to the final edge.

Your shoulders filled with ache,
I whisper into your ear,
You no longer need to wait,
You may come for me my dear.

As I drill my pet to delight,
She bursts open from the seam,
Exposing the still dark night,
Waking me from my dream.

✌ WATERFALL ✌

Baby don't you realize this effect that you have,
From wicked smile to your contagious laugh,
Only one simple touch makes me glow,
Tingling sensation from my waist below,
Acting so calm yet I feel like a clown,
You heat me up so until I must cool down.

Baby will you help me from melting away,
Come closer to me and have a 'lil play,
Treat me as a man or call me a boy,
I don't care which so long I'm your toy,
Unfasten my package and take it all,
Loving me with my back to this wall.

One thing's for sure you won't wanna bet,
I'll have you work hard to make me erect,
I need my senses to reel in infinite delight,
As we make love through the day and night,
I'm nothing like any hand-written fantasy,
Remember this as you scream in ecstasy.

Beneath this water torrent we undress,
My hands cup firmly round your breast,
Our bodies covered with flowing ripples,
As I gently bite your aching nipples,
My tongue slowly draws a sensual wake,
Your body trembles and silently quakes.

Slowly you relinquish my soul beneath,
Rasping my soft skin with your teeth,
Delicately licking my cock as it swells,
Releasing my passion from where it dwells,
Sealing my hardened length and girth,
Filling your throat as I thrust to immerse.

Lifting you up from where you now sit,
I suckle to taste nectar from your clit,
Slowly circling my firm tongue around,
Your saturated and pouring wet mound,
Grasping my long auburn hair to steady,
My tongue flicking like a deep water eddy.

As the water gently spills on my face,
Your body reaches out into space,
Slowly scratching away at the rock,
Before you feel the head of my cock,
Erotically bearing its way inside,
Steamy heat between your wet thighs.

Gallons of water cascade over your shoulder,
While I plunge into you on natures bolder,
Deafening water continues to pour,
Yet you hear my moans as I bore,
My aching shaft feels so deep inside,
Tantalizing your goddess's tide.

With my rapidly brisk hip movement,
You sense the release of my current,
Squeezing and clenching me with love,
Your body driving me to full flood,
Before you moan and begin to sway,
Amidst the perfect orgasmic wave.

Our bodies craving sexual lust,
Bursting open with reverent gust,
Flooding the plains like a burst dam,
As if the waterfall was held by a hand,
Sizzling away with our desire,
Our world of love bursting into fire.

∽ RESTRAINT ∽

Darkness surrounds us,
Seeping from my mind,
Blanketing our bodies,
As I quietly bind.

Your wrists tight together,
Hemp rope and cable ties,
With a red silk blindfold,
Your only disguise.

Upon golden shoulders,
A familiar pattern,
Black roses with diamonds,
Embossed lace upon satin.

My knuckles flex,
To touch my moist lips,
As I closely observe,
Your curvaceous hips.

Protruding from,
The blue ribbed corset,
With your erect nipple,
Clamped in my forceps.

A tiny whimper,
You try not to resist,
My muscles flex,
In my wrist.

I grasp it,
Before giving a twist,
A pinch of pain,
Between us is bliss.

PJ BAYLISS

Goddess melts away,
As if she was butter,
Your muffled growl,
Emits with a stutter.

My knuckle reappears,
Upon my lip,
With white blazing grooves,
From where I bit.

Observing you writhe,
In timeless motion,
The white caps of pain,
Stirring her ocean.

I release the restraint,
From the stainless steel tong,
Politely asking you,
If anything is wrong.

You refuse to budge,
But manage a smile,
Replying to me,
I like your style.

Nonchalantly I inspect,
Your wrists turning rare,
Bound firm and tight,
Behind your rear.

My footsteps echo,
As I casually pace,
Circling you slowly,
Admiring your lace.

Garter belt stockings,
From thigh to your heels,
With a floral suspender,
Igniting my erotic zeal.

I struggle to contain,
My excitement inside,
Slowly I'm engorged,
Thick blood in my pride.

My hand on your shoulder,
Before I come undone,
Willingly you kneel,
Suckling to become one.

The bell of my glans,
Embraces your mouth,
Your throat swells,
As I force it south.

You relish my taste,
Choking on my flesh,
While I subdue you,
My erogenous pledge.

With a fistful of hair,
I tug 'till you drool,
Pumping you hard,
As your cheeks become full.

I relinquish myself,
From the grit of your teeth,
Turning my attention,
To your goddess beneath.

She dances wildly,
Promising to shower,
As I roll into the room,
My tortuous plow.

Your heart palpitates,
As you're wrenched to your feet,
I set the black dial,
To a steady beat.

PJ BAYLISS

I flick the silk mask,
Covering your eyes,
What you now see before you,
Makes you quiver and sigh.

There in the shadows,
Lurks the machine,
Quietly humming,
Glimmering and pristine.

The black matt framing,
Stainless steel dildo,
Three-quarters of a horse,
Thrusting to and fro.

Your eyes open wide,
As I turn down the pace,
Before ripping a slice,
In your stockings of lace.

Hands remain bound,
Behind your back,
I stretch you out,
Upon wooden rack.

With a quick tug,
I secure you with rope,
Emptying your ambitions,
Filling you with hope.

My collected voice,
Rings through the air,
My every word,
Amplified through fear.

"Keep calm my lover,
You're not beyond repair,
But you may feel broken,
Once I'm done with you here."

You quiver as those words,
Slowly slip from my lips,
Before my palms part,
The lust between your hips.

Fingers upon your shoulder,
Ensuring you don't slip,
As the silver dildo,
Presses upon your clit.

Your body writhes a little,
As I slide the phallus pass,
Then tension beholds you,
As I insert it in your arse.

Shuddering with a jolt,
Against the rasping rope,
My hands upon your body,
Sensing how you cope.

Easing deep into your body,
Pain settling 'till it soothes,
Overcome with passion,
Mind drifting like a balloon.

I twist the machine dial,
Increasing speed of the thrust,
The room fills with the scent,
Of your extruded lust.

The ropes begin to tighten,
Against your only response,
Shuddering with a shock,
When I cup goddesses frond.

A sudden rush of blood,
Whirring fills the room,
As the vacuum rises,
Bringing goddess to a bloom.

PJ BAYLISS

Once again my knuckle,
Is lodged between my jaw,
Observing your convulsions,
Admiring you with awe.

Drops of sweat remind me,
And the other drops do too,
That I must indulge,
It's the only thing to do.

There is a sudden pucker,
Vacuum popping from its grasp,
Goddesses nerves are swirling,
Sensitivity makes you gasp.

As if you could have noticed,
Amidst your anguished cries,
I place the Hitachi wand,
Between your open thighs.

The silver shaft re-enters,
Time and time again,
While the intense vibrations,
Drives you round the bend.

I twist the rubber ball,
Applying pressure as I please,
Before you surge with pleasure,
Collapsing at your knees.

I bite my aching knuckle,
Turning off the pace,
Displeased at how you have,
Soaked through your black lace.

"My pet you have upset me,
I didn't say you can,
Now clean yourself up,
And we'll try this once again."

PJ BAYLISS

∾ APRIL 2013 ∾

Dear Diary,

Sometimes it's necessary to lose yourself in order to find yourself. After all, no one else will come looking if you don't appear to be missing, even if we're there in plain view of everyone.

So, is it the same principle when looking for love? Is it possible for others to see the love that is missing within us? Are we all blind to only detect passion, lust, debauchery & desire in others? Or do we misinterpret passion as always been related to sensuality as opposed to a passion to live?

I seem to have more questions at the end of my journey than I did in the beginning. I longed to be satisfied; instead, I have developed a hunger for something that cannot be filled. The more I've been fed with information, the more absent I've become…

◦— ABSENCE —◦

Every day I give up inside,
Eyes tearing up as I go and hide,
Imaging places I'd rather be,
Wishing time would set me free.

My mind spins in turmoil and pain,
Leaving me to question if I'm insane,
In desperation I submit my plea,
For this goddamned blessing to let me be.

I question & doubt my abilities,
Notions of success appear so silly,
Not another word I eventually vow,
Once again throwing in the towel.

Drafted pages drift in the breeze,
Head in my hands I begin to ease,
I shift the pain with a deep sigh,
As my beliefs drift from my eye.

So much to plan and write & do,
Will I ever see this thing through?
Will it remain just a hobby?
Will the author inside die and let me be?

I nurture my pride and take a look,
The scattered pages of the book,
Picking my path across the floor,
Leaving it behind as I shut the door.

Chains of anxiety secure my mind,
Casting me in such a bind,
To struggle on or retreat back,
Into my hole so peaceful and black.

But every now and then some light,
Reveals a path that beckons so bright,
With tippy toe I edge forward once more,
Retreating once again through my door.

Piece by piece the words unravel,
Chains break to ease me from this hell,
Finally I now edit the page,
In preparation for the empty stage.

This beast rages on inside me,
I doubt it will ever set me free,
Our battles erupt every night,
As I pick up the pen in order to fight.

∽ THE END ∽

∾ AFTERWORD ∾

This is my third poetry book, and the last I'll be writing for a while. I realize there are many readers out there that will be upset upon hearing that. However, I've reached a point in my life where I wish to turn my attention towards a new writing adventure.

Writing poetry certainly has been rewarding for me, and very challenging at times. I rely upon being in the right creative mood within a quite environment free of distraction and, on most occasions, noise. I love every aspect of writing poetry and I'm certain the odd one will slip out in the future, however I wish to write.

I intend to focus on my novel series for now: Chemical Romance. It promises to deliver a host of erotic landscapes mingled with a compelling storyline of conflict and romance. My writing mentors consider it unique, so I hope you can afford the wait and join me in my first book titled "Librium" in upcoming months.

∽ ABOUT THE AUTHOR ∾

I live in rural New Zealand surrounded by native forestry with breathtaking views of local farmland. I enjoy music and painting, but writing is my preferred hobby at this point in my life. I have an eclectic music taste and appetitive for the bizarre, which fuels my inclination to write elaborate story plots with unusual twists to keep readers intrigued.

Outside of writing, I have a career in professional consulting with experience in numerous USA fortune-500 companies, military installations, local government office, and other global ventures. For this reason I prefer to write with discretion and with strict seclusion from my author profile so as not to expose my corporate clientele.

Further details about my books, poetry, and short stories are available on the website below:

www.pjbayliss.com